See and Say
Korean

by Aerin Park

CAPSTONE PRESS
a capstone imprint

Published by Pebble, an imprint of Capstone
1710 Roe Crest Drive, North Mankato, Minnesota 56003
capstonepub.com

Copyright © 2025 by Capstone. All rights reserved. No part of this publication may be reproduced in whole or in part, or stored in a retrieval system, or transmitted in any form or by any means, electronic, mechanical, photocopying, recording, or otherwise, without written permission of the publisher.

Library of Congress Cataloging-in-Publication Data is available on the Library of Congress website.

ISBN: 9780756587413 (hardcover)
ISBN: 9780756587369 (paperback)
ISBN: 9780756587376 (ebook PDF)

Summary: How do you tell someone "You're welcome" in Korean? What's the Korean word for *Saturday*? With this book, curious kids will see and say simple words and phrases in Korean.

Editorial Credits
Editor: Ericka Smith; Designer: Sarah Bennett; Media Researcher: Svetlana Zhurkin; Production Specialist: Katy LaVigne

Image Credits
Dreamstime: Usjsn1017, 11 (top); Getty Images: ahnsungdai, 14 (middle), Imazins/k2studio, 15 (top), Imazins/KCDF, 16 (bottom right), Imazins/Plan Shoot, 8, 14 (bottom), Imazins/Plan Shooting 2, cover (bottom right), 1, 9 (bottom), 16 (bottom left), Insung Jeon, 4, phanasitti, 17 (bottom right), Multi-bits/Plan Shoot, 6, phanasitti, 17 (bottom right), Ryan McVay, 16 (top), Sanga Park, 27 (top), Sorapop, 7 (top), st_lux, 14 (top); Shutterstock: 2p2play, 19 (top right, middle), 21 (bottom left), 30042000, 17 (top right), 5 second Studio, 12 (top left), all_about_people, 7 (bottom left), anek.soowannaphoom, 22 (bottom left), asife, 31 (middle), bergamont, 29 (middle right), Boonchuay Promjiam, 29 (bottom left), Byungsuk Ko, 18 (top), CrispyPork, 12 (bottom right), D.Apiwat, 13 (bottom), DKSStyle, 20 (top), Dmitry Lobanov, 22 (top), Dragon Images, 5 (middle), 23 (bottom right), Edgunn, 10 (top), Elizabeth_0102, 29 (middle left), emre topdemir, 26 (top right), Eric Isselee, cover (middle left), 13 (middle right), FamVeld, 30 (middle left), Fascinadora, 30 (middle), Fotofermer, 28 (bottom left), Gaukhar Yerk, 23 (middle), Golfx, 7 (bottom right), gresei, cover (top right), Guitar photographer, 5 (bottom), 25 (top left, bottom right), halimqd (speech bubble and burst), cover and throughout, hoonya, 19 (bottom), Image Republic, 17 (bottom left), Irina Wilhauk, 31 (top), jindo, 12 (top right), JoannaTkaczuk, 11 (bottom), Johnathan21, 18 (middle right), Kdonmuang, 22 (bottom right), keunhyungkim, 10 (bottom), 18 (middle left), Koshiro K, 21 (bottom right), lightwavemedia, 9 (top), Magnia (lined texture), cover and throughout, Markus Mainka, 21 (top), meunierd, 21 (middle), Muenchbach, 17 (top left), Nadya Shatrova, 11 (middle right), Naypong Studio, 29 (top), Ngchiyui, 20 (bottom), nukeaf, 24, oksana2010, 28 (top right), Olga Ushakova, 11 (middle left), Olhastock, 12 (bottom left), PCPartStudio, 25 (top right), Prostock-studio, 7 (middle), PV productions, 15 (bottom), Ronnachai Palas, 23 (bottom left), Rtimages, cover (top middle), Ruth Black, 30 (top, middle right, bottom), 31 (middle right, middle left, bottom), Sorbis, 19 (top left), 20 (middle), spiharu.u (spot line art), cover and throughout, Stock for you, 26 (bottom), 27 (bottom), Sung Min, 5 (top), 10 (middle), Super Prin, 13 (top right), Superheang168, cover (bottom left), Tim UR, 28 (top left), TimeImage Production, 23 (top), TK Kurikawa, 18 (bottom), Tom Godfrey, 25 (bottom left), Tsekhmister, 13 (middle left), Vangert, 13 (top left), 28 (bottom right), VDB Photos, 26 (top left), winphong, 29 (bottom right)

Any additional websites and resources referenced in this book are not maintained, authorized, or sponsored by Capstone. All product and company names are trademarks™ or registered® trademarks of their respective holders.

Table of Contents

The Korean Language............................... 4

Greetings and Phrases............................. 6

Family... 8

Food.. 10

Animals.. 12

At Home... 14

Clothing 16

In the Neighborhood 18

Transportation 20

Hobbies 22

Days of the Week 24

Seasons 25

Weather 26

Colors.. 28

Numbers.. 30

About the Translator 32

The Korean Language

People living on the Korean peninsula have spoken the Korean language—한국어 (hahn-goo-guh) or 한국말 (hahn-goong-mahl)—since the 500s. In 1443, the Great King Sejong of the Joseon Dynasty (1392–1910) created the Korean alphabet, known as Hangul (hahn-geul). Around the world, more than 75 million people speak Korean.

Polite and Casual Conversation in South Korea
There are two ways of speaking with others—the polite way, which you use with elders, and the casual way, which you use with those your age. In Korean culture, showing respect to those older than you is expected. This book teaches you how to speak casually with people your age.

How to Use This Book

Some words and phrases create a sentence. Those will appear in bold.

English	I'm hungry. I want . . .
Korean	배고파. . . . 먹고싶다.
Say It!	bay-goh-pah. . . . muk-goh-sip-dah

+

English	breakfast.
Korean	아침
Say It!	ah-cheem

English	I like . . .
Korean	나는 . . . 좋아해.
Say It!	nah-neun . . . joh-ah-hay

+

English	dancing.
Korean	춤 추는 거
Say It!	choom choo-neun guh

Others give you the name for a person, place, thing, or idea.

English	spring
Korean	봄
Say It!	bohm

Meet Chatty Cat! Chatty Cat will show you how to say the words and phrases in this book.

5

Greetings and Phrases

| Korean | 인사말과 간단한 표현들 |
| Say It! | in-sahn-mahl-gwah gahn-dahn-hahn pyoh-hyun-deul |

English	Hello!
Korean	안녕!
Say It!	ahn-nyeong

English	My name is . . .
Korean	내 이름은 . . . 이야. (if the name ends with a consonant in Hangul)
Say It!	nay ee-leu-meun . . . ee-yah
Korean	내 이름은 . . . 야. (if the name ends with a vowel in Hangul)
Say It!	nay ee-leu-meun . . . yah

English	How are you?
Korean	잘 지내?
Say It!	jahl-jee-nay

English	I am fine.
Korean	잘 지내.
Say It!	jahl-jee-nay

English	What is your name?
Korean	이름이 뭐야?
Say It!	ee-leu-mee mwuh-yah

English	Nice to meet you.
Korean	만나서 반가워.
Say It!	mahn-nah-suh bahn-gah-woh

English Can I have this, please?
Korean 나 이거 해도 돼?
Say It! nah ee-guh hay-doh dweh

English Thank you!
Korean 고마워!
Say It! goh-mah-woh

English You're welcome!
Korean 천만에!
Say It! chun-mah-neh

English Goodbye!
Korean 잘가!
Say It! jahl-gah

English See you later!
Korean 나중에 보자!
Say It! nah-joong-eh boh-jah

English Yes.
Korean 응.
Say It! ung

English No.
Korean 아니.
Say It! ah-nee

Double Consonants

Some Korean words have double consonants, like *kk, dd, bb, ss,* and *jj*. Say the consonant's sound a little louder and with a stiffer voice for these sounds.

Family

Korean 가족
Say It! gah-johk

English This is . . .
Korean 여기는 . . .
Say It! yuh-gee-neun

English **our mother.**
Korean 우리 엄마야.
Say It! woo-lee um-mah-yah

English **our father.**
Korean 우리 아빠야.
Say It! woo-lee ahp-pah-yah

English **our younger sister.**
Korean 내 여동생이야.
Say It! nay yuh-dong-sang-ee-yah

English **our younger brother.**
Korean 내 남동생이야.
Say It! nay nahm-dong-sang-ee-yah

English **our older sister.**
Korean 우리 언니야.
(if the person speaking is a girl)
Say It! woo-lee un-nee-yah

Korean 우리 누나야.
(if the person speaking is a boy)
Say It! woo-lee noo-nah-yah

English **our older brother.**
Korean 우리 오빠야.
(if the person speaking is a girl)
Say It! woo-lee oh-pah-yah

Korean 우리 형이야.
(if the person speaking is a boy)
Say It! woo-lee hyung-ee-yah

8

English	**our aunt.**
Korean	우리 이모야. (on the mother's side)
Say It!	woo-lee ee-moh-yah
Korean	우리 고모야. (on the father's side)
Say It!	woo-lee goh-moh-yah

English	**our uncle.**
Korean	우리 외삼촌이야. (on the mother's side)
Say It!	woo-lee way-sahm-chon-ee-yah
Korean	우리 삼촌이야. (on the father's side)
Say It!	woo-lee sahm-chon-ee-yah

English	**our cousin.**
Korean	내 사촌이야.
Say It!	nay sah-chon-ee-yah

English	**our grandfather.**
Korean	우리 외할아버지야. (on the mother's side)
Say It!	woo-lee way-hah-lah-buh-jee-yah
Korean	우리 할아버지야. (on the father's side)
Say It!	woo-lee hah-lah-buh-jee-yah

English	**our grandmother.**
Korean	우리 외할머니야. (on the mother's side)
Say It!	woo-lee way-hal-muh-nee-yah
Korean	우리 할머니야. (on the father's side)
Say It!	woo-lee hal-muh-nee -yah

Food

Korean	음식
Say It!	eum-shik

> | English | I'm hungry. I want . . . |
> |---|---|
> | Korean | 배고파. . . . 먹고싶다. |
> | Say It! | bay-goh-pah. . . . muk-goh-sip-dah |

English	breakfast.
Korean	아침
Say It!	ah-cheem

English	rice balls
Korean	주먹밥
Say It!	joo-muk-bahp

English	rice porridge
Korean	죽
Say It!	jook

English	lunch.
Korean	점심
Say It!	jum-sheem

English	noodles
Korean	국수
Say It!	gook-soo

English	seaweed rice rolls
Korean	김밥
Say It!	jim-bahp

English **dinner.**
Korean 저녁
Say It! juh-nyuk

English beef bulgogi
Korean 불고기
Say It! bool-goh-gee

English **a snack.**
Korean 간식
Say It! gahn-shik

English tomato
Korean 토마토
Say It! toh-mah-toh

English milk
Korean 우유
Say It! woo-yoo

English bread
Korean 빵
Say It! bbahng

English watermelon
Korean 수박
Say It! soo-bahk

Animals

Korean 동물

Say It! dong-mool

English a dog
Korean 개
Say It! geh

English a cat
Korean 고양이
Say It! goh-yahng-ee

English a tiger
Korean 호랑이
Say It! hoh-lahng-ee

English a chicken
Korean 닭
Say It! dahk

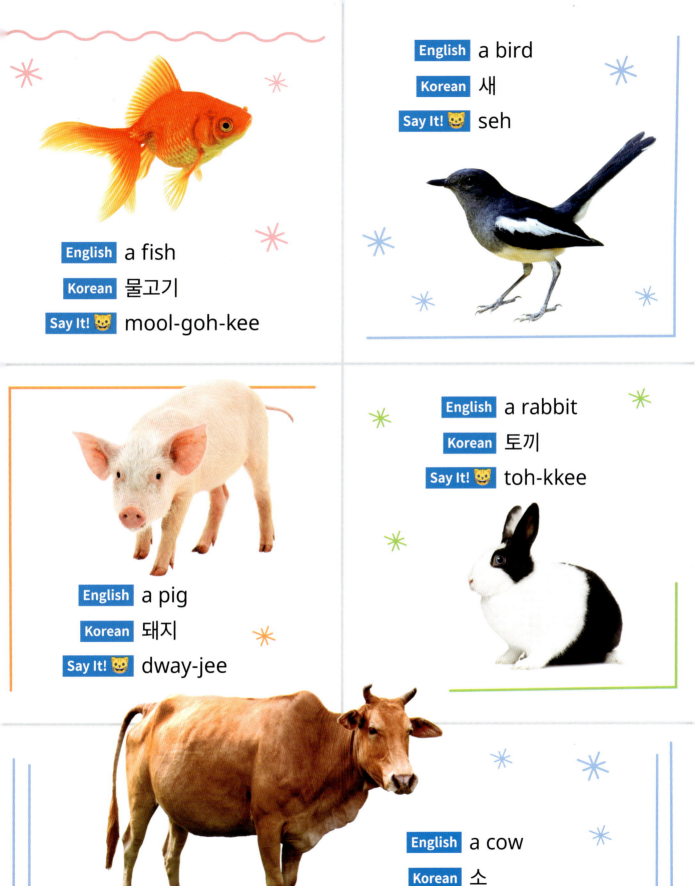

At Home

Korean 집
Say It! jeep

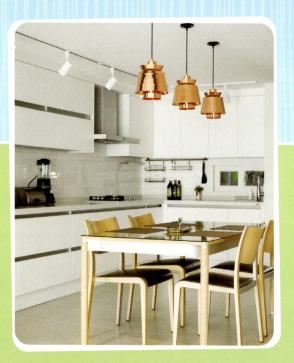

English kitchen
Korean 부엌
Say It! boo-uk

English table
Korean 식탁
Say It! shik-tahk

English chair
Korean 의자
Say It! weu-jah

English living room
Korean 거실
Say It! guh-sheel

English couch
Korean 소파
Say It! soh-pah

English cell phone
Korean 핸드폰
Say It! han-deu-pohn

English window
Korean 창문
Say It! chahng-moon

English	bedroom
Korean	방
Say It!	bahng

English	door
Korean	문
Say It!	moon

English	bed
Korean	침대
Say It!	chim-day

English	computer
Korean	컴퓨터
Say It!	kum-pyew-tuh

English	bathroom
Korean	화장실
Say It!	hwah-jahng-sheel

English	sink
Korean	세면대
Say It!	seh-myun-day

English	toilet
Korean	변기
Say It!	byuhn-gee

English	bathtub
Korean	욕조
Say It!	yok-joh

Clothing

Korean 옷
Say It! oht

English I am wearing . . .
Korean 나는 . . . 입고 있어.
Say It! nah-neun . . . ip-goh ee-ssuh

English a shirt.
Korean 셔츠
Say It! shuh-cheu

English pants.
Korean 바지
Say It! bah-jee

English I am wearing shoes.
Korean 나는 신발 신고 있어.
Say It! nah-neun shin-bahl shin-goh it-ssuh

English I am wearing a hat.
Korean 나는 모자 쓰고 있어.
Say It! nah-neun moh-jah sseu-goh it-ssuh

English hanbok.
Korean 한복
Say It! hahn-bohk

16

English a sweatshirt.
Korean 긴팔 티
Say It! keen-pahl tee

English a dress.
Korean 원피스
Say It! wuhn-pee-seu

English a skirt.
Korean 치마
Say It! chee-mah

English a coat.
Korean 코트
Say It! koh-teuh

English I am wearing socks.
Korean 나는 양말 신고 있어.
Say It! nah-neun yahng-mahl shin-goh it-ssuh

17

In the Neighborhood

Korean 동네
Say It! dong-nay

English an apartment building
Korean 아파트
Say It! ah-pah-teuh

English a park
Korean 공원
Say It! gong-wuhn

English a house
Korean 주택
Say It! joo-tayk

English a school
Korean 학교
Say It! hahk-kyoh

English a post office
Korean 우체국
Say It! woo-chay-gook

18

English	a grocery store
Korean	가게
Say It!	gah-geh

English	a library
Korean	도서관
Say It!	doh-suh-gwahn

English	a bus stop
Korean	버스 정류장
Say It!	buh-seu jeong-lyoo-jahng

English	a road
Korean	도로
Say It!	doh-loh

English	a hospital
Korean	병원
Say It!	byung-wuhn

19

Transportation

Korean	교통수단
Say It!	kyoh-tong-soo-dahn

English	a bicycle
Korean	자전거
Say It!	jah-jun-guh

English	a bus
Korean	버스
Say It!	buh-seu

English	a car
Korean	자동차
Say It!	jah-dong-chah

English	a train
Korean	기차
Say It!	kee-chah

English an airplane
Korean 비행기
Say It! bee-hang-kee

English the subway
Korean 지하철
Say It! jee-hah-chuhl

English a truck
Korean 트럭
Say It! teuh-luhk

English a boat
Korean 배
Say It! bay

Hobbies

Korean 취미
Say It! chuee-mee

English I like . . .
Korean 나는 . . . 좋아해.
Say It! nah-neun . . . joh-ah-hay

English singing.
Korean 노래하는 거
Say It! noh-lay-hah-neun guh

English playing soccer.
Korean 축구 하는 거
Say It! chook-goo hah-neun guh

English playing video games.
Korean 비디오 게임 하는 거
Say It! bee-dee-oh geh-eem hah-neun guh

English a ball
Korean 공
Say It! gong

English **reading.**
Korean 책 읽는 거
Say It! chay geek-neun guh

English a book
Korean 책
Say It! chayk

English **painting.**
Korean 그림 그리는 거
Say It! geu-leem geu-lee-neun guh

English **swimming.**
Korean 수영하는 거
Say It! soo-yung-hah-neun guh

English **dancing.**
Korean 춤 추는 거
Say It! choom choo-neun guh

23

Days of the Week

Korean 요일
Say It! yoh-eel

English Today is . . .
Korean 오늘은 . . . 이야.
Say It! oh-neu-leun . . . ee-yah

English **Monday.**
Korean 월요일
Say It! woh-ryoh-eel

English **Tuesday.**
Korean 화요일
Say It! hwah-yoh-eel

English **Wednesday.**
Korean 수요일
Say It! soo-yoh-eel

English **Thursday.**
Korean 목요일
Say It! moh-kyoh-eel

English **Friday.**
Korean 금요일
Say It! geuh-myoh-eel

English **Saturday.**
Korean 토요일
Say It! toh-yoh-eel

English **Sunday.**
Korean 일 요일
Say It! ee-ryoh-eel

24

Seasons

Korean 계절
Say It! gyeh-juhl

English spring
Korean 봄
Say It! bohm

English summer
Korean 여름
Say It! yuh-leum

English fall
Korean 가을
Say It! gah-eul

English winter
Korean 겨울
Say It! gyuh-wool

Koreans talk about the four seasons in this order: spring (March to May), summer (June to August), fall (September to November), and winter (December to February). In South Korea, the new school year starts in March, the beginning of spring.

Weather

Korean 날씨
Say It! nahl-ssee

English windy
Korean 바람 분다
Say It! bah-lahm boon-dah

English raining
Korean 비 온다
Say It! bee on-dah

English cold
Korean 춥다
Say It! choop-ddah

English snowing
Korean 눈 온다
Say It! noon on-dah

English	sunny
Korean	화창하다
Say It!	hwah-chahng-hah-dah

English	hot
Korean	덥다
Say It!	dup-ddah

English	cloudy
Korean	흐리다
Say It!	heu-lee-dah

Colors

Korean 색깔

Say It! say-kkahl

English red
Korean 빨강
Say It! bahl-gahng

English pink
Korean 분홍
Say It! boon-hong

English green
Korean 초록
Say It! choh-lohk

English orange
Korean 주황
Say It! joo-hwahng

English blue
Korean 파랑
Say It! pah-lahng

English yellow
Korean 노랑
Say It! noh-lahng

English purple
Korean 보라
Say It! boh-lah

English white
Korean 하양
Say It! hah-yahng

English black
Korean 검정
Say It! guhm-jeong

29

Numbers

Korean 숫자
Say It! soot-jah

1
English one
Korean 일
Say It! eel

2
English two
Korean 이
Say It! ee

3
English three
Korean 삼
Say It! sahm

4
English four
Korean 사
Say It! sah

5
English five
Korean 오
Say It! oh

The Korean language has two numbering systems. Sino-Korean numbers are used for dates, money, calculations, and phone numbers. Native Korean numbers are used for counting, including age. The numbers below are Sino-Korean numbers.

6

English six
Korean 육
Say It! yook

7

English seven
Korean 칠
Say It! cheel

8

English eight
Korean 팔
Say It! pahl

9

English nine
Korean 구
Say It! goo

10

English ten
Korean 십
Say It! sip

31

About the Translator

Aerin Park, born and raised in South Korea, believes that language is a bridge to people's stories, culture, and history. She is passionate about integrating these elements into her work—both translation and Korean language teaching. When she's not working, you will find Aerin sharing Korean history with her three children, making kimchi from garden veggies, and shoveling Minnesota snow.